CONTENTS

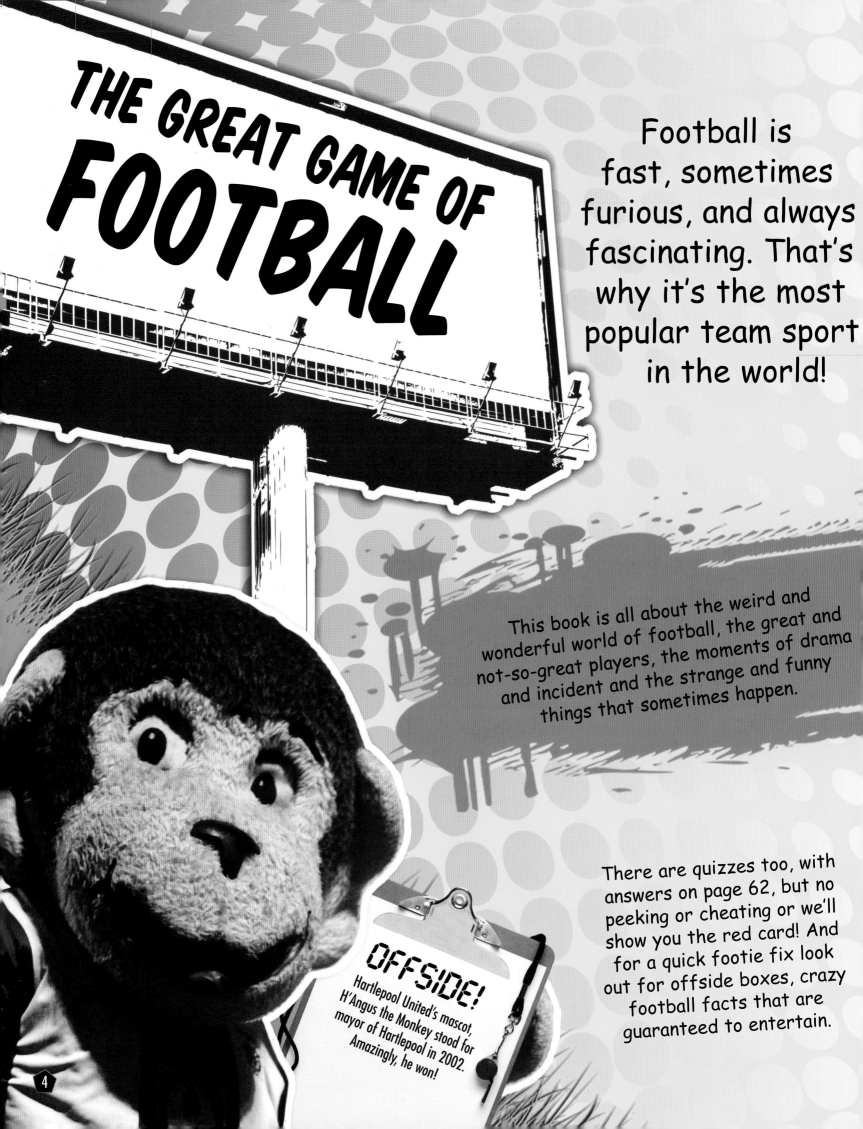

THE GREAT GAME OF FOOTBALL

Football is fast, sometimes furious, and always fascinating. That's why it's the most popular team sport in the world!

This book is all about the weird and wonderful world of football, the great and not-so-great players, the moments of drama and incident and the strange and funny things that sometimes happen.

There are quizzes too, with answers on page 62, but no peeking or cheating or we'll show you the red card! And for a quick footie fix look out for offside boxes, crazy football facts that are guaranteed to entertain.

There are quizzes too, with answers on page 62

OFFSIDE!

Hartlepool United's mascot, H'Angus the Monkey stood for mayor of Hartlepool in 2002. Amazingly, he won!

4

KICK OFF!

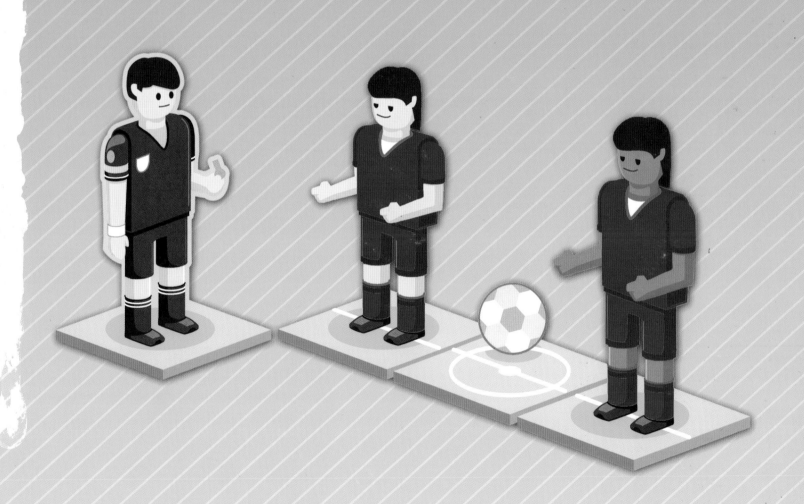

CLIVE GIFFORD

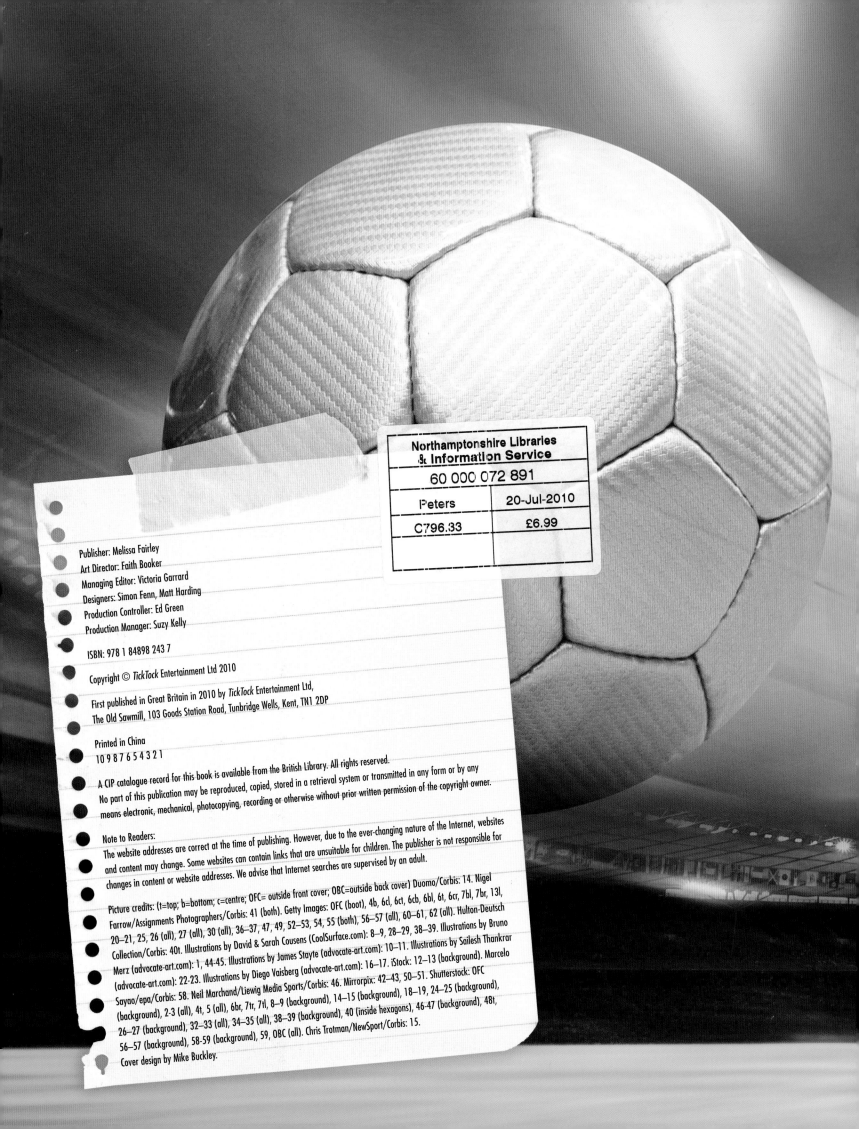

Publisher: Melissa Fairley
Art Director: Faith Booker
Managing Editor: Victoria Garrard
Designers: Simon Fenn, Matt Harding
Production Controller: Ed Green
Production Manager: Suzy Kelly

ISBN: 978 1 84898 243 7

Copyright © TickTock Entertainment Ltd 2010

First published in Great Britain in 2010 by TickTock Entertainment Ltd,
The Old Sawmill, 103 Goods Station Road, Tunbridge Wells, Kent, TN1 2DP

Printed in China
10 9 8 7 6 5 4 3 2 1

Note to Readers:
The website addresses are correct at the time of publishing. However, due to the ever-changing nature of the Internet, websites
and content may change. Some websites can contain links that are unsuitable for children. The publisher is not responsible for
changes in content or website addresses. We advise that Internet searches are supervised by an adult.

Picture credits: (t=top; b=bottom; c=centre; OFC= outside front cover; OBC=outside back cover) Duomo/Corbis: 14. Nigel
Farrow/Assignments Photographers/Corbis: 41 (both). Getty Images: OFC (boot), 4b, 6cl, 6ct, 6cb, 6bl, 6t, 6cr, 7bl, 7br, 13l,
20–21, 25, 26 (all), 27 (all), 30 (all), 36–37, 47, 49, 52–53, 54, 55 (both), 56–57 (all), 60–61, 62 (all). Hulton-Deutsch
Collection/Corbis: 40t. Illustrations by David & Sarah Cousens (CoolSurface.com): 8–9, 28–29, 38–39. Illustrations by Bruno
Merz (advocate-art.com): 1, 44-45. Illustrations by James Stayte (advocate-art.com): 10–11. Illustrations by Sailesh Thankrar
(advocate-art.com): 22-23. Illustrations by Diego Vaisberg (advocate-art.com): 16–17. iStock: 12–13 (background). Marcelo
Sayao/epa/Corbis: 58. Neil Marchand/Liewig Media Sports/Corbis: 46. Mirrorpix: 42–43, 50–51. Shutterstock: OFC
(background), 2-3 (all), 4t, 5 (all), 6br, 7tr, 7tl, 8–9 (background), 14–15 (background), 18–19, 24–25 (background),
26–27 (background), 32–33 (all), 34–35 (all), 38–39 (background), 40 (inside hexagons), 46-47 (background), 48t,
56–57 (background), 58-59 (background), 59, OBC (all). Chris Trotman/NewSport/Corbis: 15.

Cover design by Mike Buckley.

RECIPE FOR SUCCESS

For a good game of football you need 11 players on each side, a football, a pitch, goals and a referee to make sure everyone plays fairly.

YOU NEED A PITCH to play football on. In 1990, Kotor and Bokeljan, two teams in Yugoslavia's third division, turned up to play their match only to find their pitch had been taken over by a circus. The two teams were allowed in free to watch!

THE REFEREE IS IN CHARGE of running a football match smoothly. Well, usually. Brian Savill was refereeing a match when he got carried away: he ran over to the ball and scored a goal!

OVER 40 MILLION FOOTBALLS are sold every year. In one game in the 1930 World Cup, Argentina and Uruguay both insisted on playing one half of the match with their own ball.

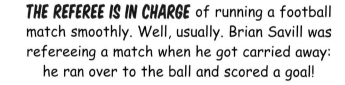

THE BALL HAS TO TRAVEL BETWEEN THE GOALPOSTS for a goal to be scored. In 1999, Danny Worthington of the Stalybridge Celtic Colts scored an unusual goal. His pass bounced off a passing seagull and the ball ended up in the net. Don't worry though, the seagull flew away dazed but not injured!

A WINNING TEAM

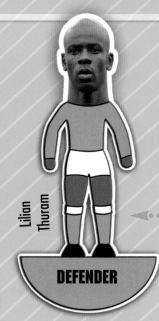

Lilian Thuram has played over 100 times for France. He scored two goals in the 1998 World Cup semi-final against Croatia – not bad for a defender!

Lilian Thuram

DEFENDER

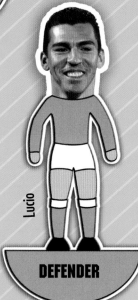

Ronald Koeman

Defenders help stop the other team from scoring goals. Some defenders score them, too. Dutch defender Ronald Koeman scored an amazing 193 league goals for clubs including Barcelona and Ajax.

DEFENDER

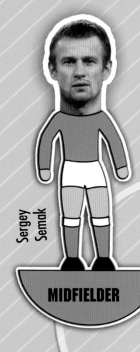

Sergey Semak

MIDFIELDER

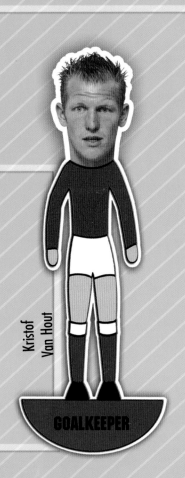

Kristof Van Hout

GOALKEEPER

Goalkeeper Kristof Van Hout is the tallest professional footballer in the world. He stands a gigantic 2.08m tall in his football socks.

Lucio

Brazilian central defender Lucio has played for Bayern Munich in Germany and Inter Milan in Italy's Serie A. He played every minute of Brazil's 2002 World Cup Finals campaign which saw them crowned world champions.

DEFENDER

Veteran Italian defender Paolo Maldini helped AC Milan win the Champions League in 2007 – exactly 40 years after his Dad, Cesare Maldini, had done so. Paolo's two sons play for AC Milan's youth team!

Paolo Maldini

DEFENDER

Top midfielders are very well paid by their football club sponsors. According to *France Football* magazine, David Beckham earned over £28 million in 2008.

David Beckham

MIDFIELDER

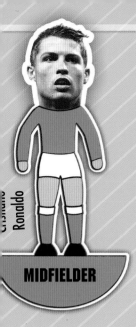

MIDFIELDER

Cristiano Ronaldo

Wide midfielders who attack down the sideline are called wingers. Cristiano Ronaldo can strike the ball at speeds of over 120km/h – faster than some cars!

Midfielders have to run a lot in a football match. In four games at Euro 2008, Russian midfielder Sergey Semak ran an incredible total of 50.03km.

Wayne Rooney

STRIKER

Strikers are a team's most lethal goalscorers. Playing for Liverpool Schoolboys, 11-year-old Wayne Rooney scored over 70 goals in just 28 games.

Frank Lampard

MIDFIELDER

Frank Lampard has scored over 110 goals – more than any other midfielder in the Premier League. Bet you didn't know that Frank has an A grade GCSE in Latin, or that his first goal in the English league was for Swansea City in 1995.

Jürgen Klinsmann

STRIKER

With 11 World Cup strikes, 47 goals for the German national team and over 300 goals throughout his club career, many for Tottenham Hotspur, Jürgen Klinsmann was a true goal machine.

Every winning football team is a blend of players with ifferent talents and skills. Here's a talented team of 11 and some amazing facts about each team member.

TERRIFIC TEENAGERS

3 RYAN GIGGS

When he was 14, Ryan Giggs was told he wasn't good enough to play for Manchester City's youth team. Instead he joined Manchester United and went on to play over 800 times for the team. That's more than any other player.

2 IDRISS KAMENI

Cameroon's goalkeeper at the 2000 Olympics was 16-year-old Idriss Kameni. He saved lots of goals, Cameroon won and he became the youngest ever Olympic football gold medallist.

1 PELÉ

Pelé played for Brazil when he was just 16. A year later he became the youngest player in a World Cup Final. He scored twice as Brazil beat Sweden 5-2, making him the youngest ever goalscorer.

4 FERNANDO TORRES

In a big 2004 game in Spain, Fernando Torres captained his Athletico Madrid side against Real Madrid. He was only 19 at the time.

5

FREDDY ADU

Freddy Adu first appeared for Major League Soccer (MLS) team, DC United when he was 14 years old.

7

ELENA DANILOVA

Elena Danilova is the youngest goalscorer at the Women's World Cup. She scored for Russia in 2003 at the age of 16.

9

PETER OFORI-QUAYE

The youngest ever Champions League goalscorer was Peter Ofori-Quaye who scored for Olympiakos at the age of 17 years and 194 days.

6

LIONEL MESSI

Lionel Messi was signed by Barcelona when he was just 13 years old. He and his family moved from Argentina to Spain.

8

THEO WALCOTT

Theo Walcott was the youngest player at the 2006 World Cup – he had just turned 17. He is also England's youngest ever player.

10

MAURICIO BALDIVIESO

In 2009, Mauricio Baldivieso played his first match for top Bolivian team, Aurora. He was just 12 years old, so not even a teenager!

TOP TEN RED FACES

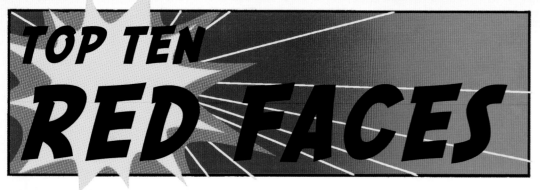

Sometimes football can leave you red-faced and with the blues. Here are ten mortifying moments which left players or managers very embarrassed.

1. Someone Needs Glasses

German coach Ralf Rangnick was left red-faced after screaming at a very lazy player. He suddenly realized it was the referee he had been shouting at!

2. Speedy Strike

ZOOM!

WHOOSH!

8.3 SECONDS

The fastest goal in international football was scored by Davide Gualtieri for minnows, San Marino. Who were the embarrassed team who let in a goal after just 8.3 seconds? England!

3. Problem Pants

Giuseppe Meazza went to take a penalty for Italy in the 1938 World Cup semi-final when his shorts fell down.

Meazza coolly pulled his shorts up, held on to them ... and scored! Italy went on to win the World Cup.

4. Babayaro's Boo-Boo

BOiING!

Nigerian defender Celestine Babayaro was playing for Chelsea when he celebrated a team-mate's goal with a spectacular somersault.

CRASH!

The injury it caused meant he was out for three months!

5. Kit Trick

Losing 3-0 to Southampton in 1996, Alex Ferguson ordered his Manchester United players to remove their unlucky and embarrassing away shirts. The grey kit was never worn again.

6. HENRY'S HOWLER

Thierry Henry was playing for Arsenal when he scored the winner against Chelsea in a 2000 Premier League game.

He celebrated by hitting the corner flag which rebounded back into his face.

Poor Thierry had to get treatment from the trainer. The opposition fans looked on and laughed!

7. DIABY'S DISASTER

Own goals are when a player scores in his own team's goal. Arsenal's Abou Diaby's own goal in 2009 gave rivals Manchester United a 2-1 win in the Premier League.

8. STAN'S THE MAN

If Diaby was upset imagine how defender Stan Van Den Buys felt. His side lost 3-2 to Anderlecht in 1995. All three of Anderlecht's goals were own goals scored by him!

9. SPRAKE'S MISTAKE

It was a long time ago – back in 1967 – but goalkeeper Gary Sprake scored a classic own goal. He went to throw the ball out, slipped and threw the ball into his own net!

10. WHOOPS, IT'S A WINGER

It's not just male footballers who make mistakes. England winger Sue Smith went to take a corner but instead of kicking the ball, she kicked the corner flag and fell in a heap. Oops!

GREAT SAVE!
THE TOP TEN GOALKEEPERS

1

LEV YASHIN

This Russian great was so great that FIFA created the Lev Yashin Award for the best goalkeeper at a World Cup. Yashin has saved more than 150 penalties during his career.

2

DINO ZOFF

The oldest ever World Cup-winning captain, Dino Zoff, was 40 when he lifted the trophy in 1982. Zoff held the record for the most minutes in international games without letting in a goal, a whopping 1,142 minutes or 12 matches in a row.

3

GORDON BANKS

Banks was England's goalie when they won the World Cup in 1966. At the 1970 World Cup he made possibly the greatest save in history when he clawed a Pelé header over the bar.

4

GIANLUIGI BUFFON

In 2001, Buffon became the world's most expensive keeper when Italian club Juventus paid £32 million for him. He helped Italy win the 2006 World Cup.

5

SEPP MAIER

A World Cup winner with Germany, Maier is remembered for his enormous gloves and his great goalkeeping. Over 11 years, he played 422 games in a row without being dropped.

6

PETER SCHMEICHEL

Huge and scary, Schmeichel is thought of as one of the best goalkeepers of the 1990s. He captained Denmark 30 times and won many trophies with Manchester United.

7
IKER CASILLAS

Casillas started playing in goal for the mighty Real Madrid when he was just 18. A year later, he became the youngest-ever goalkeeper to play in a Champions League final.

8
MOHAMED AL-DEAYEA

Mohamed Al-Deayea has played more matches for his country than any other goalkeeper. He appeared at three World Cups and played 181 times for Saudi Arabia.

9
PETER SHILTON

Shilton played for England a record 125 times, keeping 66 clean sheets. Over 30 years, he played for 11 different clubs totalling 1,005 English league games.

10
EDWIN VAN DER SAR

Van der Sar has won 130 caps for the Netherlands, more than any other player.

Peter Schmeichel

TOP TEN FEMALE FOOTBALLERS

Mia Hamm

2

MARTA

Three times winner of the World Player of the Year award, Brazilian Marta has won four Swedish championships with her club Umea.

3

BIRGIT PRINZ

Prinz is the women's World Cup highest scorer and has scored 122 goals for Germany. She was nearly signed by Italian men's club Perugia!

4

KRISTINE LILLY

No footballer, male or female, has played more times for her country than Lilly who has made 340 appearances for Team USA.

1

MIA HAMM

The youngest ever player when she first appeared for the US national team at age 15, Hamm would dominate women's football in the 1990s and onwards. She has scored 158 international goals.

KELLY SMITH

Smith scored 30 goals for Arsenal in one season. She's famous for the 2009 winner against Russia – an outrageous 40-metre lob.

PERPETUA NKWOCHA

Nigeria's star midfielder, Nkwocha has led her country to three African championships and has also appeared at the Olympics and two World Cups.

TIFFENY MILBRETT

In 2005, Milbrett scored her 100th goal for the USA while playing Ukraine in her home town of Portland.

HANNA LJUNGBERG

Ljungberg first played for Sweden at the age of 17 in an 8-0 thrashing of Spain. She scored an incredible 10 goals at the 2003 World Cup.

HEGE RIISE

The Norwegian defender played in a boys' team for eight years before winning the 1995 Women's World Cup and the 2000 Olympics gold medal.

BRIANA SCURRY

USA's star goalkeeper for 15 years, Scurry won two Olympic gold medals and in 1999, helped USA win the Women's World Cup.

Hanna Ljungberg

15

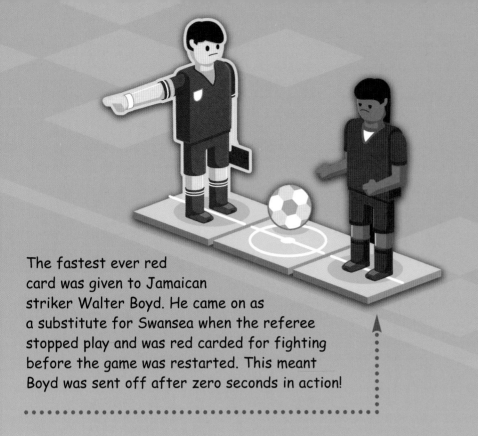

The fastest ever red card was given to Jamaican striker Walter Boyd. He came on as a substitute for Swansea when the referee stopped play and was red carded for fighting before the game was restarted. This meant Boyd was sent off after zero seconds in action!

The red card we see today was only invented in the 1960s. The first player to be shown a red card at a World Cup was Chile's Carlos Caszely in 1974.

There have been 172 red cards shown during World Cup games. France's Zinedine Zidane and Cameroon's Rigobert Song are the only players to have been sent off more than once.

English referee Martin Sylvester showed himself the red card after he lost his temper during an amateur game in 1998.

'OFF!'
RED CARD REACTIONS

In 2005, Newcastle players Kieron Dyer and Lee Bowyer were both shown the red card, but not for fighting their opponents – they were fighting each other!

Carlton Palmer has been sent off for five different English League clubs – Sheffield Wednesday, Southampton, Leeds United, Coventry and Nottingham Forest.

In 2009, referee Jose Manuel Barro Escandón sent off a staggering 19 players in a match in Spain.

When the referee showed Fernando d'Ercoli the red card in an Italian game in 1990, he grabbed the card and ate it!

And the most red cards in one game? It is believed to be in Paraguay in 1993 when the referee sent off 20 of the 22 players for fighting.

THE WORST
THRASHINGS

A THRASHING MEANS LOSING BY LOTS OF GOALS. IT HAPPENS TO ALL TEAMS. EVEN MANCHESTER UNITED HAVE LOST 7-0 THREE TIMES. WHEN YOUR SIDE LOSES BADLY, GIVE A THOUGHT TO THE FOLLOWING TEAMS WHO WERE ON THE END OF SOME OF THE BIGGEST THRASHINGS IN FOOTBALL.

AUSTRALIA 31 - 0 AMERICAN SAMOA

THE BIGGEST THRASHING IN WORLD CUP QUALIFYING HISTORY. ARCHIE THOMPSON SCORED 13 TIMES DURING THIS 2001 MATCH.

ARBROATH 36 - 0 BON ACCORD

IN THIS 1885 SCOTTISH CUP MATCH, ARBROATH SCORED 15 GOALS IN THE FIRST HALF AND 21 IN THE SECOND. IT COULD HAVE BEEN WORSE – ARBROATH HAD FIVE GOALS DISALLOWED.

OLYMPOS XYLOFAGOU 24 - 3 AYIOS ATHANASIOS

IN A 2007 LEAGUE MATCH IN CYPRUS, OLYMPOS XYLOFAGOU BEAT
AYIOS ATHANASIOS 24-3. OLYMPOS STRIKER PANAGIOTIS PONTIKOS
BAGGED AN INCREDIBLE 16 GOALS IN THE GAME.

HUNGARY 6 - 3 ENGLAND

IT MAY NOT LOOK LIKE MUCH OF A THRASHING, BUT ENGLAND'S 6-3
LOSS AT WEMBLEY TO HUNGARY IN 1953 WAS HUGE. ENGLAND HADN'T
LOST TO A TEAM FROM OUTSIDE BRITAIN OR IRELAND FOR 52 YEARS.

NETHERLAND ANTILLES 14 - 0 PUERTO RICO

PUERTO RICO PLAYED SIX MATCHES AGAINST OTHER COUNTRIES IN 1946 AND THE
TWO MATCHES THEY LOST 4-1 WERE THEIR SMALLEST DEFEATS. THEY LOST 6-0
TO VENEZUELA, 12-1 TO PANAMA, 12-0 TO COSTA RICA AND 14-0 TO THE
NETHERLAND ANTILLES! ALL FOUR GAMES TOOK PLACE IN THREE TERRIBLE WEEKS.

PENAROL 12 - 2 THE STRONGEST

URUGUAYAN TEAM, PENAROL SECURED THE BIGGEST VICTORY IN SOUTH
AMERICA'S COPA IBERTADORES, WINNING 12-2. THEIR BOLIVIAN OPPONENTS
WERE CALLED THE STRONGEST. THEY CLEARLY WEREN'T.

CHINA 22 - 0 MALAYSIA

THE 2006 ASIAN U19 TOURNAMENT SAW CHINA
THRASH MALAYSIA, THE HOST NATION, 22-0.

TOP LEAGUE HOT SHOTS

Top football clubs play in leagues in their own country. Here are the top scorers in the four biggest leagues in the world.

SPANISH LA LIGA

1. Telmo Zarra 251
2. Hugo Sánchez 234
3. Alfredo di Stéfano 227
4. César Rodríguez Álvarez 226
5. Raúl 224

ENGLISH PREMIER LEAGUE

1. Alan Shearer 260
2. Andrew Cole 187
3. Thierry Henry 174
4. Robbie Fowler 163
5. Les Ferdinand 149

ITALIAN SERIE A LEAGUE

1. Silvio Piola 274
2. Gunnar Nordahl 225
3. José Altafini 216
4. Giuseppe Meazza .216
5. Roberto Baggio 205

GERMAN BUNDESLIGA

1. Gerd Müller 365
2. Klaus Fischer 268
3. Jupp Heynckes 220
4. Manfred Burgsmüller 213
5. Ulf Kirsten 181

Alan Shearer

GREAT GOAL CELEBRATIONS

ROBOT DANCER

1.
2.

After being caught dancing like a robot at a party at David Beckham's house, Peter Crouch performed a robot dance after scoring for England against Hungary and Jamaica in the summer of 2006.

A PANTS CELEBRATION

1.
2.

In 2007, Manchester City midfielder Stephen Ireland scored against Sunderland. To celebrate he dropped his shorts to show off his Superman underpants to the crowd. Amazingly, he escaped with only a telling off.

THE MEXICAN SOMERSAULT

1.
2.
3.
4.

Hugo Sanchez was a Mexican striker who scored hundreds of goals in Spain for teams like Real Madrid in the 1980s.

Taught how to backflip and somersault by his sister who was a gymnast, Sanchez was one of the first to perform acrobatic goal celebrations.

Brazilian striker, Bebeto, had just become a dad when he scored at the 1994 World Cup. He celebrated by pretending to rock a baby in front of the crowd. Team-mates joined in and a popular goal celebration for new footballing fathers was born.

1.

2.

Facundo Sava was a striker from Argentina who hid a mask in his football socks. If he scored, he would pull out the mask and wear it to look like Zorro or the Lone Ranger!

THE SHEARER

1.

2.

No fuss, just run away with your right arm up in the air. That's what Alan Shearer did every time he scored, and he scored a lot for England and for his various clubs. He is the English Premier League's leading goalscorer with 260 goals.

At the 1990 World Cup, Cameroon's Roger Milla entertained the crowd when he ran to the corner flag and wiggled his hips to do a little dance. The Milla wiggle became one of the most famous video clips of the World Cup.

Aylesbury United are nicknamed the Ducks. When they score, the team drop to their knees, flap their arms and waddle in a line. Quackers!

WHAT'S THE SCORE?

1. In the 2007/08 season, how many goals did Cristiano Ronaldo score for Manchester United?

A) 42

B) 37

C) 31

2. How many goals did the Brazilian striker Pelé score in the 1959 season?

A) 48

B) 66

C) 127

3. San Marino have let in more goals trying to qualify for the European Championship than any other team. How many?

A) 100

B) 200

C) 300

4. Bobby Charlton is England's leading goalscorer in international games. How many goals did he score?

A) 38

B) 49

C) 57

5. Jimmy McGrory played for Celtic and Clydebank and scored more goals in the Scottish league than any other player. How many?

A) 410

B) 236

C) 198

6. German striker Miroslav Klose scored five times at the 2002 World Cup. How many of them were headers?

A) 2
B) 5
C) None

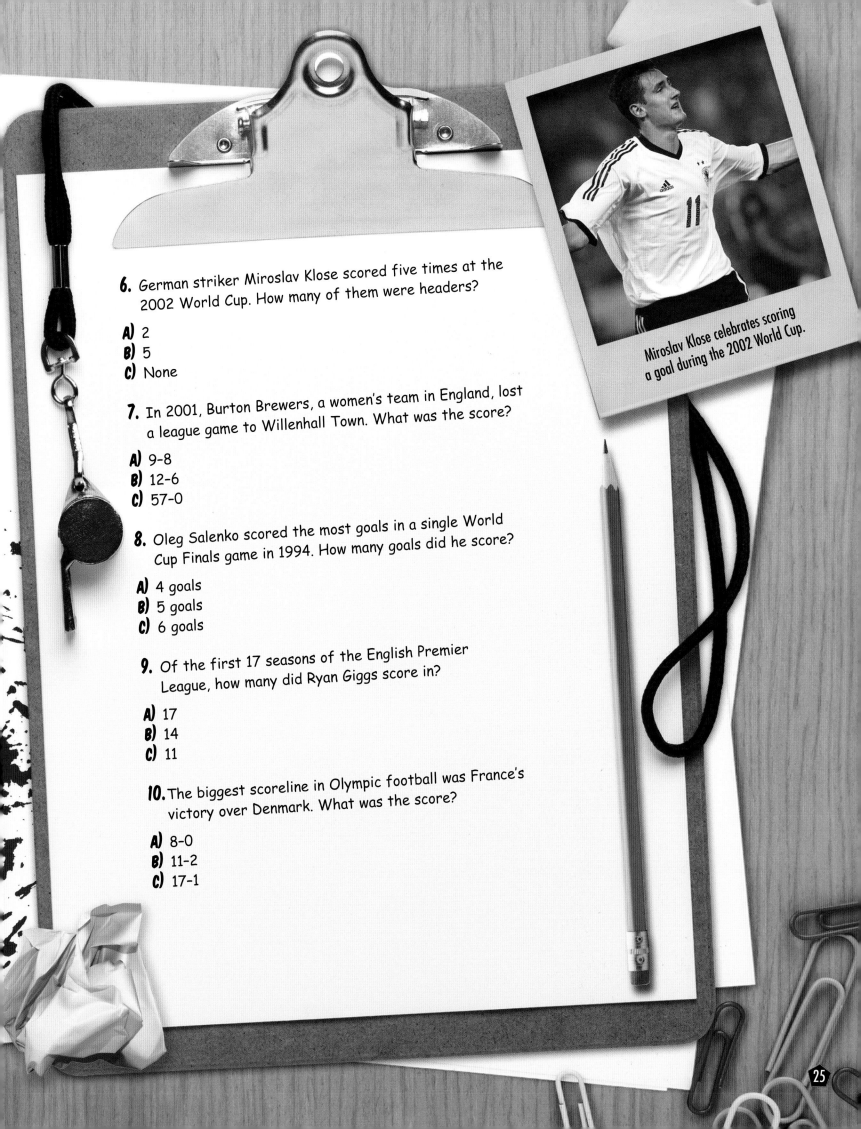

Miroslav Klose celebrates scoring a goal during the 2002 World Cup.

7. In 2001, Burton Brewers, a women's team in England, lost a league game to Willenhall Town. What was the score?

A) 9-8
B) 12-6
C) 57-0

8. Oleg Salenko scored the most goals in a single World Cup Finals game in 1994. How many goals did he score?

A) 4 goals
B) 5 goals
C) 6 goals

9. Of the first 17 seasons of the English Premier League, how many did Ryan Giggs score in?

A) 17
B) 14
C) 11

10. The biggest scoreline in Olympic football was France's victory over Denmark. What was the score?

A) 8-0
B) 11-2
C) 17-1

TOP GOALSCORING GOALKEEPERS

ROGÉRIO CENI

With 84 goals under my belt, I'm the ultimate goalscoring goalie. I've played for Brazil 17 times and for Brazilian club São Paulo over 700 times. When I've scored, my team always wins!

JOSÉ LUIS FÉLIX CHILAVERT

I'm brilliant under pressure – many of my 64 goals were scored in crucial matches. In 1999, I became the first goalkeeper to score a hat-trick for my club Velez Sarsfield.

RENE HIGUITA

I'm a bit of a showman. I'm known for my spectacular and sometimes crazy saves. Bet you didn't know that I've scored 41 goals in professional football, including eight for my country, Colombia?

It's the goalkeepers' job to stop goals, but they occasionally score them as well. They head up the pitch in the last seconds of a game to try to score a winner or take a penalty or free kick. Here's a round-up of the best goalscoring goalies.

JORGE CAMPOS

Do you like my jersey? I designed it myself! I'm from Mexico and have played for my country over 140 times. I've scored 40 fantastic goals and even convinced my boss at Pumas to let me play as striker!

HANS-JÖRG BUTT

I'm Hans and I'm a handy hot-shot from the penalty spot. All 26 of my goals in the German league have been penalties. After a season in Portugal with Benfica, I joined Bayern Munich in 2008.

100 GOALS

80 GOALS

60 GOALS

40 GOALS

20 GOALS

0 GOALS

WONDER GOALS

Everyone has an opinion on the best goals ever scored. Here are a few crackers. Apologies if your favourite isn't here.

60M!

UESATO, 2009

Kazumasa Uesato plays in Japan's J-League. His amazing long range goal was scored with a shot from inside his own half, over 60m away from goal. Kazumasa even slipped as he struck the ball.

IBRAHIMOVIÇ, 2004

Zlatan Ibrahimoviç was playing for Ajax against NAC Breda when he scored this awesome goal. Twisting and turning, he seemed to beat the whole Breda team before pretending to shoot, changing direction and then calmly slotting the ball into the net.

Zlatan dazzles the defenders.

SINCLAIR, 1997

While playing for QPR against Barnsley in 1997, Trevor Sinclair had his back to goal as the ball raced high across the pitch. He leapt up and performed the perfect overhead scissors kick from just outside the penalty area. The goalie didn't stand a chance!

Tricky Trev's sensational shot was voted goal of the season by BBC viewers.

Ronaldo shoots . . . Ronaldo scores!

RONALDO, 1997

Brazilian striker Ronaldo avoided eight opposition defenders to run 55m and score a classic goal for Barcelona in the Spanish league.

MARADONA, 1986 WORLD CUP

Diego Maradona turned a complete circle to get away from two England defenders. Still in his own half of the pitch, he weaved his way past many of the England team to score an epic goal.

Maradona works his magic.

HALF TIME

HAIR TODAY, GONE TOMORROW

Some footballers have made some serious hairdressing decisions with hilarious results. Can you match the hairstyle to the famous international footballer?

1. Carlos Valderrama

2. Taribo West

3. Alexi Lalas

4. Jason Lee

5. Abel Xavier

A.

B.

C.

D.

E.

The referee blows his whistle for half time. Have a breather. You deserve it. Here are some some silly jokes and fun quizzes for you to enjoy during the 15 minute interval.

Which famous goalkeeper can jump higher than a crossbar?

ALL OF THEM. A CROSSBAR CAN'T JUMP!

'My football team's ground is the only place where you can't have a tea or coffee. The reason is all the mugs are on the pitch and we've never won a cup.'

Why was the rubbish footballer known as Cinderella?

BECAUSE HE KEPT RUNNING AWAY FROM THE BALL!

Did you hear about the footballer who burped?

HE SAID HE WAS SORRY, IT WAS A FREAK HIC!

OUCH!

Football injuries are not normally a laughing matter, but here are eight funny injuries that happened away from the pitch. Can you match the player to the injury?

PLAYERS

1. Santiago Cañizares (Spain's goalkeeper)

2. Alex Stepney (Manchester United goalkeeper)

3. Robbie Keane (Irish striker)

4. Kevin Keegan (England striker)

5. Svein Grondalen (Norwegian defender)

6. Milan Rapaiç (Croatian striker)

INJURIES

A. Poked his flight boarding pass in his eye.

B. Toe injured by being stuck in a bath tap.

C. Dislocated his jaw whilst shouting at his team-mates.

D. Collided with a moose whilst out jogging.

E. Ruptured his knee when stretching for the TV remote control.

F. Damaged foot tendons after dropping a bottle of aftershave on his foot and missed the 2002 World Cup as a result.

TOP TEN RICHEST FOOTBALL CLUBS

FOOTBALL CLUB	INCOME IN THE 2007/08 SEASON
1. Real Madrid	£365.8 million
2. Manchester United	£324.8 million
3. FC Barcelona	£308.8 million
4. Bayern Munich	£295.3 million
5. Chelsea	£268.9 million
6. Arsenal	£264.4 million
7. Liverpool	£210.9 million
8. AC Milan	£209.5 million
9. AS Roma	£175.4 million
10. Inter Milan	£172.9 million

OFFSIDE!

People were shocked when Manchester United paid £12.24 million for Ronaldo, an unknown teenager from Portugal, in 2003. Six years later, however, the club made over £67 million profit when the skilful winger was sold to Spanish giants Real Madrid.

Cristiano Ronaldo

NAME GAME

Can you figure out the original name of ten famous football clubs?

Match the original club name to the current one.

ORIGINAL NAME

1. ARDWICK AFC
2. DIAL SQUARE
3. DONOSTIA CF
4. NEWTON HEATH
5. PRIMA HAM FC
6. ST DOMINGO FC
7. ST JUDE'S
8. THAMES IRONWORKS FC
9. TORPEDO-ZIL
10. TOYOTA FOOTBALL CLUB

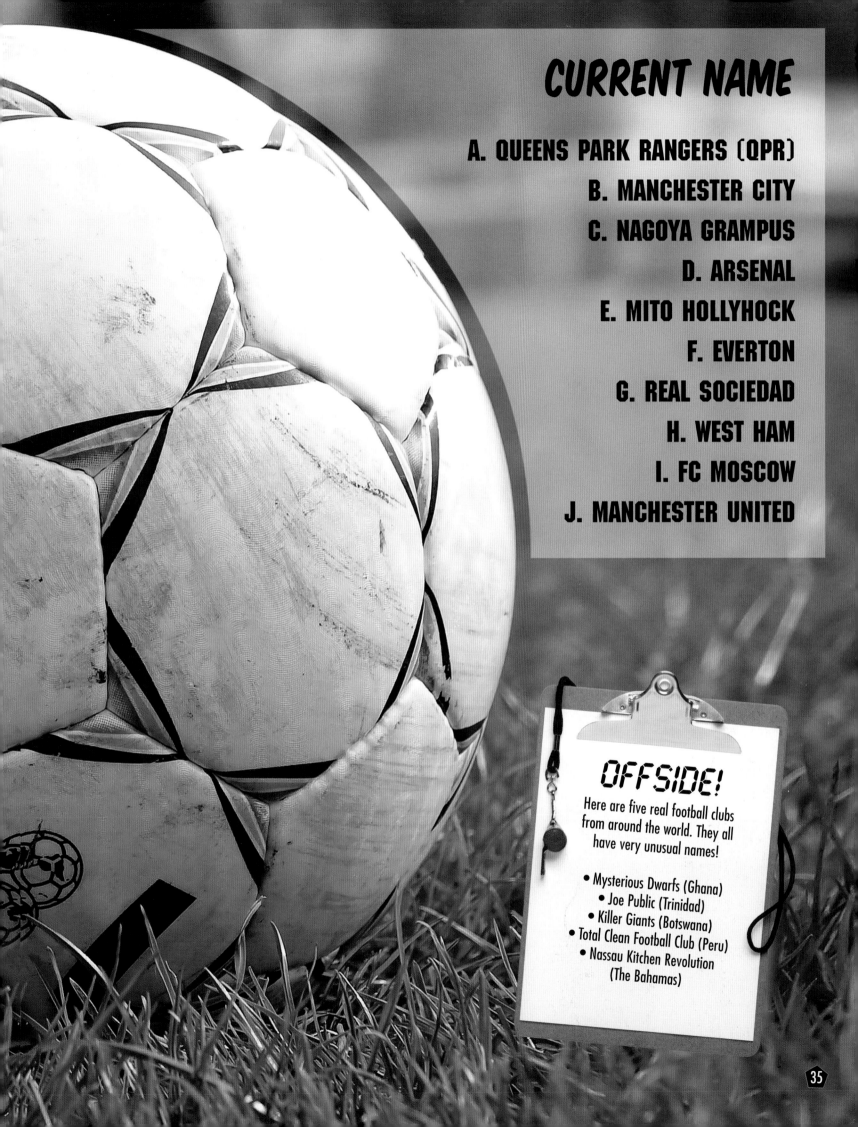

CURRENT NAME

A. QUEENS PARK RANGERS (QPR)

B. MANCHESTER CITY

C. NAGOYA GRAMPUS

D. ARSENAL

E. MITO HOLLYHOCK

F. EVERTON

G. REAL SOCIEDAD

H. WEST HAM

I. FC MOSCOW

J. MANCHESTER UNITED

OFFSIDE!

Here are five real football clubs from around the world. They all have very unusual names!

- Mysterious Dwarfs (Ghana)
- Joe Public (Trinidad)
- Killer Giants (Botswana)
- Total Clean Football Club (Peru)
- Nassau Kitchen Revolution (The Bahamas)

TOP TEN CHAMPIONS
LEAGUE CLUBS

The biggest competition for clubs in Europe is the European Cup. It began in 1956 but became the UEFA Champions League in 1992. Here are the competition's ten most successful clubs.

FOOTBALL CLUB	WINS	RUNNERS-UP
1. Real Madrid	9	3
2. AC Milan	7	4
3. Liverpool	5	2
4. Bayern Munich	4	3
5. Ajax	4	2
6. Barcelona	3	3
7. Manchester United	3	1
8. Juventus	2	5
9. Benfica	2	5
10. Inter Milan	2	2

Lionel Messi of Barcelona scores against Manchester United in the 2009 UEFA Champions League Final.

TOP TEN BIGGEST TRANSFERS

£30.8 MILLION

10 — ANDRIY SHEVCHENKO

TRANSFERRED FROM AC MILAN TO CHELSEA IN 2006

£32.5 MILLION

8 — ROBINHO

TRANSFERRED FROM REAL MADRID TO MANCHESTER CITY IN 2008

£35.7 MILLION

6 — HERNÁN CRESPO

TRANSFERRED FROM PARMA TO LAZIO IN 2000

£32.0 MILLION

9 — CHRISTIAN VIERI

TRANSFERRED FROM LAZIO TO INTER MILAN IN 1999

£32.6 MILLION

7 — GIANLUIGI BUFFON

TRANSFERRED FROM PARMA TO JUVENTUS IN 2001

Here are the largest transfers in world football.

ZINÉDINE ZIDANE

TRANSFERRED FROM JUVENTUS TO REAL MADRID IN 2001

£46.7 MILLION

4

ZLATAN IBRAHIMOVIĆ

TRANSFERRED FROM INTER MILAN TO BARCELONA IN 2009

£60.7 MILLION

THE £20 MILLION STRIKER SAMUEL ETO'O WAS ALSO PART OF THE TRANSFER DEAL

2

LUÍS FIGO

TRANSFERRED FROM BARCELONA TO REAL MADRID IN 2000

£37.0 MILLION

5

KAKÁ

TRANSFERRED FROM AC MILAN TO REAL MADRID IN 2009

£56.0 MILLION

3

CHRISTIANO RONALDO

TRANSFERRED FROM MANCHESTER UNITED TO REAL MADRID IN 2009

£80 MILLION

1

TRANSFER FREE!

Okay, well not quite free, but transfer fees don't always reach the millions. Here are ten unusual transfer fees.

Can you match the fee to the footballer?

Dixie Dean

TRANSFER FEES

1. 550 beef steaks

2. 30 tracksuits

3. £3,000

4. A set of weights

5. £200 and a bag of footballs

6. A set of football kits

7. 15kg of pork sausages (best quality, mind)

8. A freezer full of ice cream

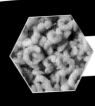

9. The player's weight in fresh shrimp

10. £200 and 35 litres of beer

Zat Knight

TRANSFER TARGETS

A. ERNIE BLENKINSOP

Left back and England captain when they beat Spain 7-1. He played 26 times for his country.

B. KENNETH KRISTENSEN

Norwegian striker who was transferred in 2002.

C. LUTEL JAMES

Manchester-born striker who moved to English Championship side Bury FC in 1998.

D. MARIUS CIOARA

Romanian midfielder who moved to Regal Hornia in 2006.

E. HUGHIE McLENAHAN

Midfielder who played 112 league matches for Manchester United.

F. IAN WRIGHT

England and Arsenal striker who first made his name when he moved to Crystal Palace in 1985.

G. DANIEL ALLENDE

All-action player who was transferred between Uruguay's top two professional teams.

H. ZAT KNIGHT

Tall central defender who moved to Fulham in 1999 and has played twice for England.

I. JOHN BARNES

Famous Liverpool winger who played 79 times for England.

J. DIXIE DEAN

Legendary goalscorer who scored 349 league goals for Everton in total.

John Barnes

Pelé

TOP TEN INTERNATIONAL GOALSCORERS

Footballers play international matches when they play for their country's team. Here are the leading goalscorers in international matches.

1. Ali Daei (Iran) ....109 goals in 149 games

2. Ferenc Puskás (Hungary and Spain) .....84 goals in 89 games

3. Pelé (Brazil) ....77 goals in 92 games

4. Bashar Abdullah (Kuwait) ....75 goals in 134 games

5. Sándor Kocsis (Hungary) ....75 goals in 68 games

6. Stern John (Trinidad and Tobago) ......69 goals in 109 games

7. Hossam Hassan (Egypt) ....69 goals in 169 games

8. Gerd Müller (West Germany) ....68 goals in 62 games

9. Majed Abdullah (Saudi Arabia) ....67 goals in 139 games

10. Kiatisuk Senamuang (Thailand) ....65 goals in 130 games

BETTER THAN BOYS

The leading female goalscorers have outscored the men. Team USA's Mia Hamm has scored a staggering 158 goals while her team-mate Kristine Lilly has scored 129. Birgit Prinz is catching up with them. She has already scored 125 goals for Germany.

TOP TEN BIG LEAGUES

Each country's football clubs compete in their national league. Footballers from all over the world come to play in the biggest leagues.

1. SPAIN — LA LIGA

Most La Liga championships won: Real Madrid, 31. Real Madrid and Barcelona have both scored over 5,000 goals in La Liga since it was formed in 1929.

2. ITALY — SERIE A

Most Serie A championships won: Juventus, 27. There's big money in Italy. The first £100,000, one million, five million, ten million and thirty million pound players in the world were all bought by Italian Serie A clubs.

3. GERMANY — BUNDESLIGA

Most Bundesliga championships won: Bayern Munich, 31.

4. ENGLAND — PREMIER LEAGUE

Most Premier League championships won: Liverpool and Manchester United, 18.

5. FRANCE — LIGUE 1

Most Ligue 1 championships won: AS Saint-Étienne, 10.

6. ARGENTINA — PRIMERA DIVISIÓN

Most Primera División championships won: River Plate, 33.

7. BRAZIL — CAMPEONATO BRASILEIRO DA SÉRIE A

Most Campeonato Brasileiro da Série A championships won: São Paulo, 10.

8. UNITED STATES — MAJOR LEAGUE SOCCER

Most Major League Soccer championships won: D.C United, 4.

9. JAPAN — J-LEAGUE

Most J-League championships won: Tokyo Verdy, 7.

10. WOMEN'S PROFESSIONAL SOCCER

Most Women's Professional Soccer championships won: Los Angeles Sol, 1. This league has just started and is based in the United States. Cristiane from Brazil scored the league's first hat-trick.

OFFSIDE!

The African Champions League is a competition for Africa's top club sides. It began in 1964. Egyptian teams Al-Ahly and Zamalek have won it 11 times while the 2009 Champions were TP Mazembe from the Democratic Republic of Congo.

FOOTBALL CRAZY

Here are ten outrageous or ridiculous events from around the world. Which are true and which are false?

1. Leopold Kielholz scored three goals for Poland in the 1934 World Cup while wearing glasses.

True or False?

2. David Beckham's first league goal was scored for Preston North End.

True or False?

3. Cameroon footballer Samuel Eto'o was once transferred for 25 footballs.

True or False?

4. Portuguese winger Cristiano Ronaldo's left foot is insured for £150 million.

True or False?

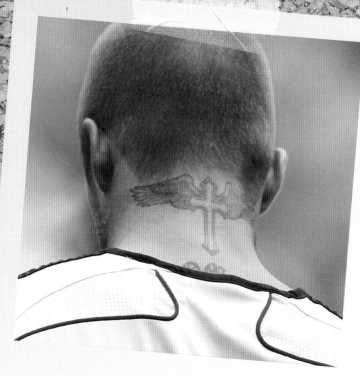

5. David Beckham once played a game in Spain in a large hat to keep the rain off his new neck tattoo.

True or False?

6. Welsh goalkeeper Leigh Roose wore a lucky shirt under his goalie top which he didn't wash for 20 years.

True or False?

7. Brazilian striker Pelé scored 90 hat-tricks in his career.

True or False?

8. Scottish player Tommy Ross scored the world's fastest hat-trick in just 90 seconds.

True or False?

9. The most own goals scored in any one match was 149 in Madagascar.

True or False?

10. The Indian team failed to turn up at the 1950 World Cup because they wanted to play in bare feet and weren't allowed.

True or False?

OFFSIDE!

When Dutch manager Co Adriaanse's team, Willelm II, lost 6-1 to Gent in 1999, he was so angry that he ordered his team to drive to a village 13km away from their ground. He took all their car keys and ordered them to jog all the way home, collect their keys and then jog all the way back to their cars!

TOP TEN EURO FACTS

National teams in Europe compete in the European Championships every four years. The men's competition began in 1958, while the women's tournament first took place in 1984.

1 The Denmark national team had failed to qualify for Euro '92 and were all on holiday when they were offered a last-minute place. Despite being completely unprepared, they beat Germany 2-0 in the final to become unexpected champions.

2 During the 1988 European Championships, Marco van Basten was on the edge of the penalty area, almost by the goal line. As the ball flew over, he thumped it into the corner of the goal. It is considered to be one of the greatest Euro goals ever.

3 At the 1968 tournament, Italy and the Soviet Union drew their semi-final game. As there were no penalty shootouts back then, Italy went through to the final simply by guessing a coin toss correctly.

4 Greece were expected to get thrashed during Euro 2004. They had never won a game at a European Championship, or indeed a World Cup, before. Yet, amazingly, they beat France, the Czech Republic and Portugal twice to win the competition.

5 France's Michel Platini is the Euro's leading goalscorer. He scored all of his nine goals during the 1984 tournament - not bad for a midfielder.

6 Germany lead the way as European champions. They have won three men's championships and an incredible seven out of ten women's tournaments. At the Women's European final in 2009, Germany beat England 6-2.

7 During Euro 2000 a Dutch fan was arrested by police for painting the entire house he was renting in his team's colours – bright orange!

8 Including qualifying matches, Spain have scored the most goals in European Championships – a total of 272. At the 2008 tournament they scored 12 goals and beat Germany in the final. They hadn't won a major football competition since 1964.

9 In 2008 Germany racked up the biggest score in European Championship history. They mauled San Marino 13-0 during a qualifier, with Lukas Podolski scoring four of the goals.

10 Iceland 10 – 0 Portugal. That amazing scoreline was the result of a qualifying match for the 2001 Women's European Championship. It remains Iceland's biggest football victory ever.

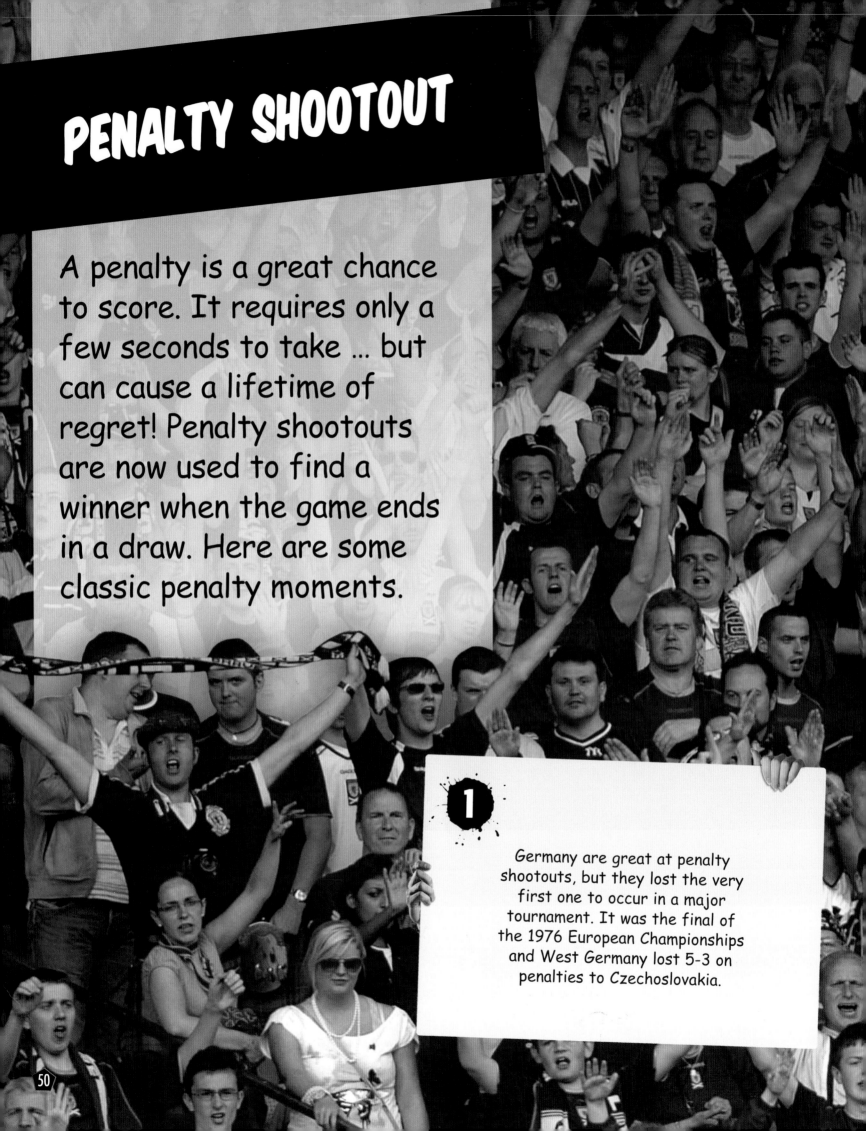

PENALTY SHOOTOUT

A penalty is a great chance to score. It requires only a few seconds to take ... but can cause a lifetime of regret! Penalty shootouts are now used to find a winner when the game ends in a draw. Here are some classic penalty moments.

1

Germany are great at penalty shootouts, but they lost the very first one to occur in a major tournament. It was the final of the 1976 European Championships and West Germany lost 5-3 on penalties to Czechoslovakia.

2

The referee ordered Kilmarnock's Tommy White to retake a penalty SEVEN times. On the seventh attempt White's kick was saved by the Partick Thistle goalkeeper.

4

Some penalty shootouts take a long time. When KK Palace and Civics played in the Namibia Cup in 2005 they needed a whopping 48 penalties to decide on a winner.

3

Martin Palermo had a terrible time in an international match against Colombia. He took three penalties for Argentina during the game. The first hit the post, the second missed the goal completely and the third was saved. Argentina lost.

5

Italian footballer Roberto Baggio became the first footballer to 'lose' the World Cup in a penalty shootout when he blazed the ball over the bar at the 1994 tournament.

TOP TEN
WORLD CUP TEAMS

Team	World Cup Winners	Runners-up	Total Games	Wins	Draws	Losses
1. Brazil	5	2	92	64	14	14
2. Italy	4	2	77	44	19	14
3. Germany	3	4	92	55	19	18
4. Argentina	2	2	65	33	13	19
5. Uruguay	2	0	40	15	10	15
6. France	1	1	51	25	10	16
7. England	1	0	55	25	17	13
8. Netherlands	0	2	36	16	10	10
9. Czechoslovakia	0	2	30	11	5	14
10. Hungary	0	2	32	15	3	14

The Soccer City Stadium in Johannesburg, South Africa –
the host stadium of the 2010 FIFA World Cup Final.

The FIFA World Cup is held every four years and began in 1930. It is the BIGGEST football tournament, but only seven countries have ever won it.

DAILY KICK OFF

HAIL CESAR!

Slovenia 1-0 Italy (2004)

Bostjan Cesar became a Slovenian hero when his 82nd minute goal beat the mighty Italy during this 2006 qualifier. Italy would recover to win the World Cup.

WORLD CUP SHOCKS

Omam-Bikick of Cameroon scores the winning goal against Argentina.

Cameroon 1-0 Argentina (1990)

Argentina were the World Cup holders and had Diego Maradona, the world's best player, in their team. Cameroon, the underdogs, were down to just nine men but still managed to win a very famous victory.

Germany 11 Argentina 0 (2007)

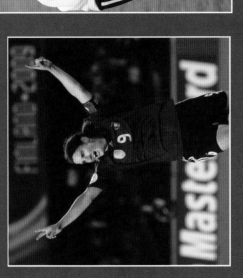

Sandra Smisek

Yes, you're reading that right. The German women's team ran riot against Argentina at the 2007 World Cup with Sandra Smisek and Birgit Prinz both scoring hat-tricks.

Birgit Prinz

Switzerland 1-2 Luxembourg (2008)

Luxembourg had won only one match in 13 years before playing this 2010 World Cup qualifying away match. Switzerland had appeared at Euro 2008, but Luxembourg still managed to beat them in a shock win.

Algeria 2-1 West Germany (1982)

The West Germans were one of the favourites to win the 1982 tournament, while Algeria were considered no-hopers who were playing their first ever World Cup. The result made history.

Senegal 1-0 France (2002)

The 1998 World Cup winners started the 2002 tournament expecting to beat Senegal. Papa Bouba Diop's goal proved them wrong, however, and gave the African team an amazing victory.

United States 1-0 England (1950)

England losing to the United States doesn't sound a big deal today but at the time England were one of the best teams in the world and many of the US team were only part-time players. When the score reached Britain, many people thought it was a misprint and the real score was actually 1-10 to England!

Bolivia 6-1 Argentina (2009)

The match took place on 1 April but the score was no April Fool's Day joke. Bolivia, who have never won a game at a World Cup, and only qualified for two of the 17 tournaments, thrashed Argentina in a 2010 qualifier. Joaquin Botero was the hero with a hat-trick.

Northern Ireland 1-0 Spain (1982)

Northern Ireland were the smallest country to qualify for the World Cup in 1982. They were playing the hosts and were reduced to ten men. Everything was stacked against them ... until Gerry Armstrong scored and Northern Ireland triumphed.

ROTTEN TOMATOES FOR TEAM ITALIA

North Korea 1-0 Italy (1966)

Italy's entire team were shamefaced when they lost to a North Korean team at the World Cup they were expected to win. The team was pelted with tomatoes when they returned to Italy.

THE TOP WORLD CUP GOALSCORERS

Gerd Müller
(Germany)
14 GOALS

Ronaldo
(Brazil)
15 GOALS

Juste Fontaine
(France)
13 GOALS

Pelé
(Brazil)
12 GOALS

Jürgen
Klinsmann
(Germany)
11 GOALS

There have been 2,063 goals scored at men's World Cup tournaments. Here are the leading goal scorers.

Sándor Kocsis
(Hungary)
11 GOALS

Teófilo
Cubillas
(Peru)
10 GOALS

Gabriel
Batistuta
(Agentina)
10 GOALS

Gary Lineker
(England)
10 GOALS

Helmut Rahn
(Germany)
10 GOALS

1. How many red cards were shown at the 2006 World Cup?

2. How many seconds did it take Hakan Sukur to score the World Cup's fastest goal?

3. How many national teams made their first appearance at a World Cup tournament in 2006?

4. The smallest crowd at a World Cup game was the Peru v Romania match in 1930. How many were in the crowd?

5. What was the average age in years of the Nigerian team who played in the 1991 Women's World Cup?

6. How many goals have Brazil scored in all the men's World Cup tournaments?

7. How many minutes did Walter Zenga play in goal for Italy during World Cups without letting in a goal?

8. How many goals have been scored during qualifying tournaments for the men's World Cups?

9. How many seconds was substitute Ebbe Sand of Denmark on the pitch before he scored against Nigeria in 1998?

10. What is the highest ever attendance for a Women's World Cup match?

Kaka

THE WORLD CUP NUMBERS GAME

Here's a World Cup puzzler to finish the book with. All you have to do is match the correct number from below to the questions on the left.

GOOD LUCK!

FULL TIME

Well, the referee has blown the whistle for the end of the game and the end of this book.

We hope you enjoyed reading about some of the impressive and downright silly things that have happened in football.

If you want to find out more, try some of these books and websites.

BOOKS

The Kingfisher Football Encyclopedia
Clive Gifford, Kingfisher Publications

Foul Football
Michael Coleman, Scholastic

How to Improve at Football
Jim Drewett, TickTock Books

Clash Football World Cup
Clive Gifford, TickTock Books

WEBSITES

www.goalkeepersaredifferent.com/
A great website about goalkeepers that features lots of amazing facts.

http://www.fifa.com/worldfootball/statisticsandrecords/
This website is packed with stats and records from the World Cup and other big tournaments.

http://news.bbc.co.uk/sport1/hi/football/default.stm
Keep up with all the latest football news at the BBC website.

www.kidsjokes.co.uk/jokes/sports
Have a giggle at the football jokes on this website.

EXTRA TIME
ANSWERS

PAGES 24–25:
WHAT'S THE SCORE?

1A	2C
3B	4B
5A	6B
7C	8B
9A	10C

PAGES 30–31: HALF TIME
Hair today, gone tomorrow

1D Carlos Valderrama

2E Taribo West

3C Alexi Lalas

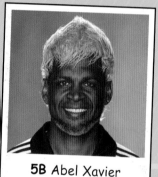

4A Jason Lee

5B Abel Xavier

PAGES 34–35: NAME GAME
1B Ardwick AFC = Manchester City
2D Dial Square = Arsenal
3G Donostia CF = Real Sociedad
4J Newton Heath = Manchester United
5E Prima Ham FC = Mito Hollyhock
6F St Domingo FC = Everton
7A St Jude's = Queens Park Rangers
8H Thames Ironworks FC = West Ham United
9I Torpedo-ZIL = FC Moscow
10C Toyota Football Club = Nagoya Grampus

PAGES 30–31: HALF TIME
Ouch!

1F Santiago Cañizares dropped a bottle of aftershave on his foot.

2C Alex Stepney dislocated his jaw shouting at his team-mates.

3E Robbie Keane ruptured his knee stretching for the TV remote.

4B Kevin Keegan got his toe stuck in the bath tap.

5D Svein Grondalen collided with a moose whilst jogging.

6A Milan Rapaiç poked his eye with his flight boarding card.

PAGES 40–41: TRANSFER FREE!
1G 550 beef steaks – Daniel Allende
2H 30 tracksuits – Zat Knight
3J £3,000 – Dixie Dean
4F A set of weights – Ian Wright
5C £200 and a bag of footballs – Lutel James
6I A set of football kits – John Barnes
7D 15kg of pork sausages (best quality, mind) – Marius Cioara
8E A freezer full of ice cream – Hughie McLenahan
9B The player's weight in fresh shrimp – Kenneth Kristensen
10A £200 and 35 litres of beer – Ernie Blenkinsop

PAGES 46–47: FOOTBALL CRAZY

1. True. He scored 13 goals for Poland in total.
2. True.
3. False.
4. False.
5. False. But he did have a new neck tattoo when he played the game.
6. True and poooo!
7. True. What a striker.
8. True. He scored the goal for Ross County in 1964.
9. True. AS Adema v Stade Olympique L'Emyrne, Madagascar in 2002.
10. True, honestly.

PAGES 58–59: THE WORLD CUP NUMBERS GAME
1. 28 **2.** 11 **3.** 6 **4.** 300
5. 18 **6.** 201 **7.** 517,
8. 14,127 **9.** 16 **10.** 90,185

GLOSSARY

attendance
The number of fans at a football ground watching a match.

clean sheet
When no goals are scored against a team during a match.

disallowed
When the ball has gone into the goal but the referee chooses not to count it as a real goal because of a foul or some other issue.

FIFA
FIFA is short for Fédération Internationale de Football Association. It is the organization that runs all world football, including the World Cup.

hat-trick
When one player scores three goals in a game.

kick off
Apart from being the name of the great book you are reading, this is how each half of a football match is started. The ball is kicked forward from the centre spot of the pitch.

penalty
A kick from the penalty spot just over 11 metres from the goal. A referee might award a penalty to a team who have been fouled inside the penalty area or if there has been a deliberate handball.

penalty area
A rectangular area marked out on a pitch around each goal.

professional
A person who is paid to play football as a job.

qualifying games
The matches played in order to decide which teams enter a competition, for example, the World Cup.

red card
Shown by a referee to signal that a footballer is being sent off and must leave the pitch. His or her team must play on with one less player.

semi-final
Two matches played in a competition like the World Cup. The winners of each semi-final play each other in the final.

substitute
A player who comes on during the game to replace a team-mate who is tired, injured, not playing well, or because the manager wants his team to play in a different way.

transfer fee
The sum of money or goods paid by one club to buy a footballer from another club.

veteran
An older, more experienced footballer.

INDEX